THIS BOOK BELONGS TO:

____

____

____

All inquiries about this book can be sent to the author at
info@dianealber.com
Published in the United States by Diane Alber Art LLC
ISBN 978-0-9912482-5-4
For more information or to book an event, visit our website:
www.dianealber.com
Printed in China

TO MY CHILDREN, RYAN AND ANNA

NEVER UNDERESTIMATE THE POWER OF TEAMWORK.

THIS IS A STORY OF A COLORFUL CREW.

MADE FROM PAINT SPLATTERS OF RED, YELLOW, AND BLUE.

EACH OF THEM HAD AN ARTISTIC FLAIR,

WITH SPLOTCHES AND BLOTCHES AND SPIKY, WET HAIR.

BUT THIS CREW WAS DIFFERENT FROM MOST THAT YOU'D SEE.
THEY EACH WORKED ALONE, NOT TOGETHER AS THREE.
ONE COLOR PER DRAWING IS HOW THEY'D EACH PLAY,
NEVER KNOWING THERE COULD BE A MUCH BETTER WAY.

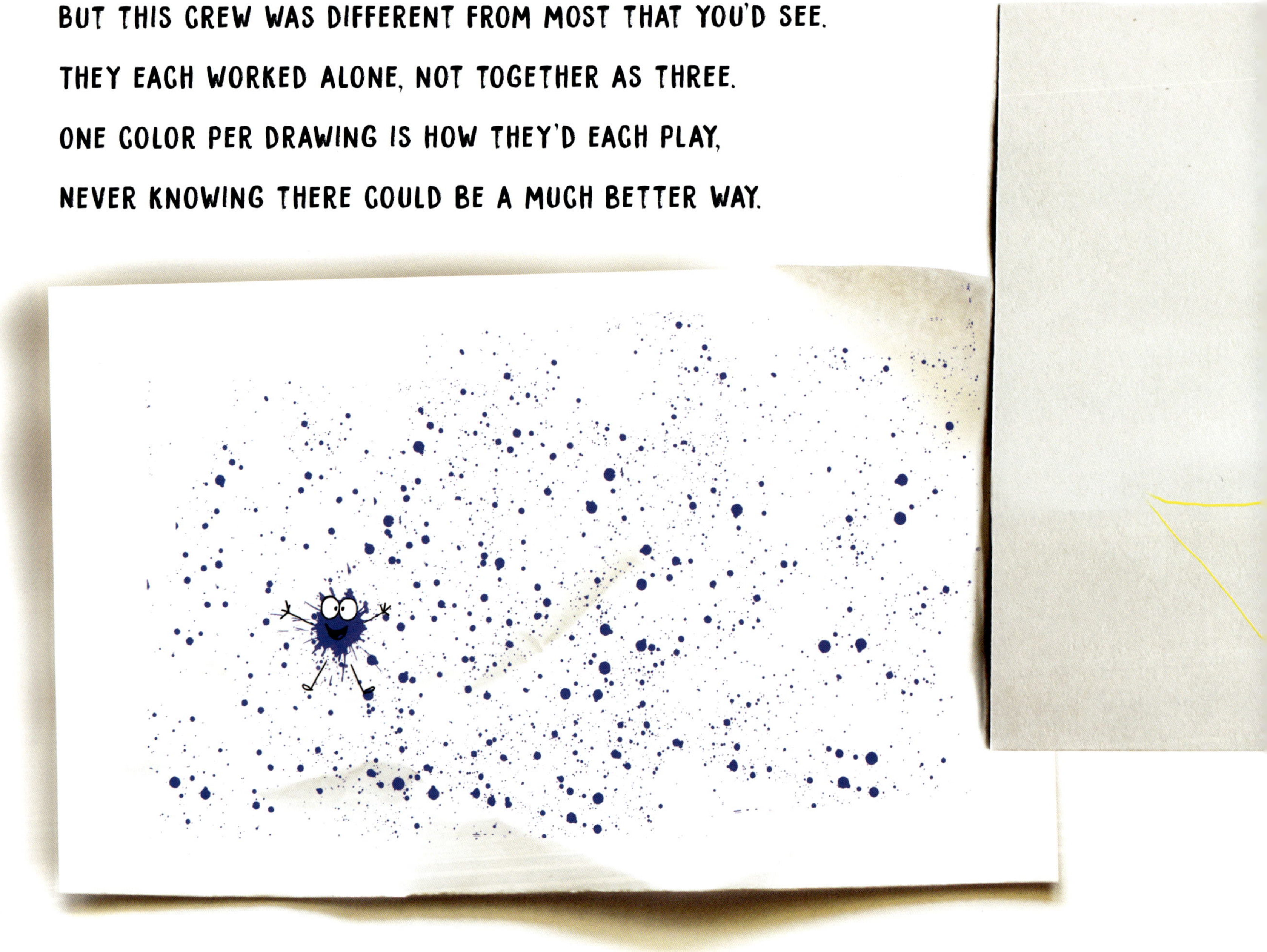

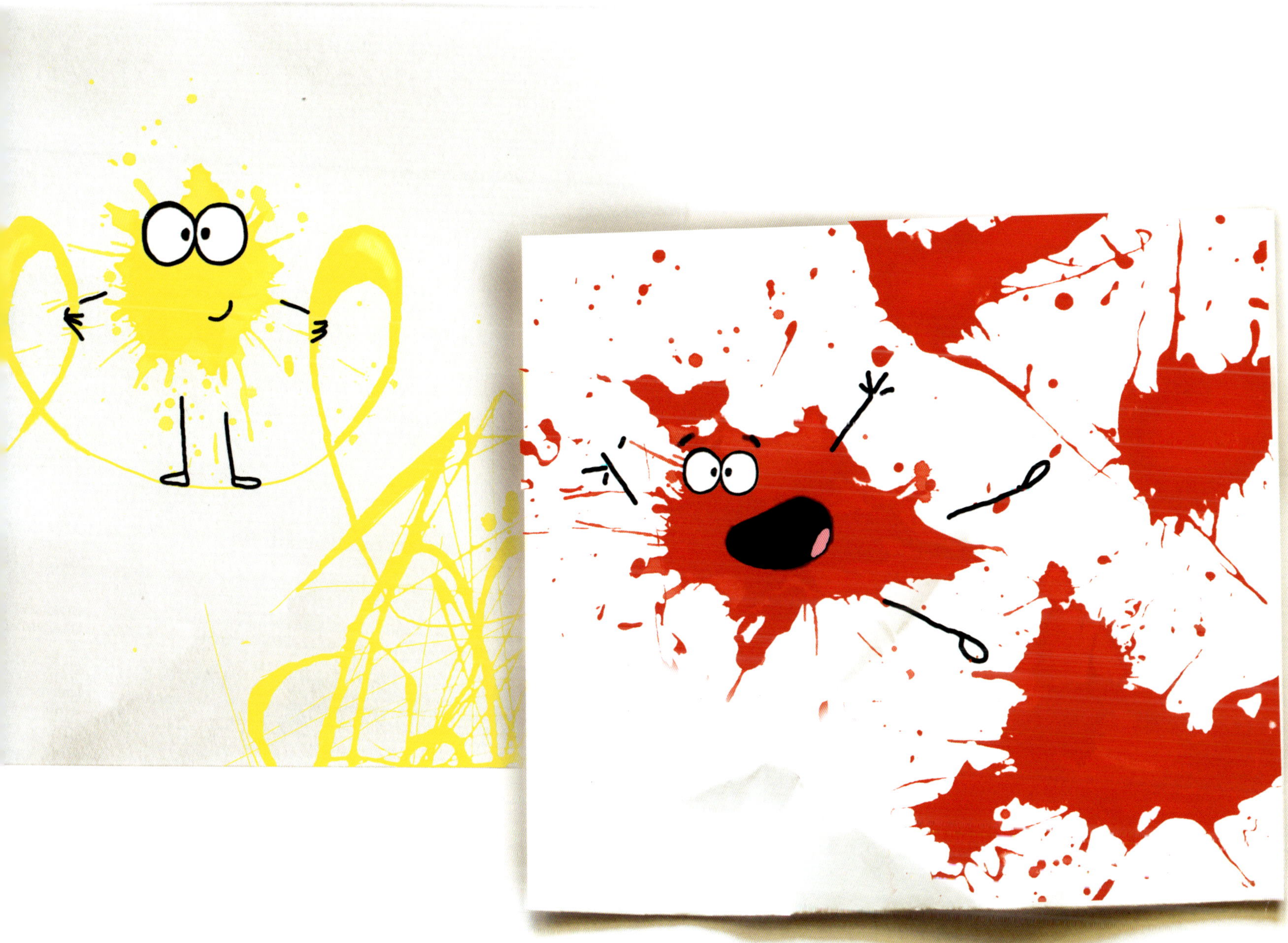

THEN ONE LOVELY MORNING, RED GATHERED THE CREW
AND SAID WITH EXCITEMENT, "LET'S TRY SOMETHING NEW!
INSTEAD OF US PAINTING SO FAR APART,
WHY DON'T WE WORK ON THE SAME PIECE OF ART?"

THEY LOVED THE IDEA AND YELLED OUT, "WE'RE IN!
WHAT DO WE DO FIRST? WHERE DO WE BEGIN?"
THEY WERE SO HAPPY THEY ALL COULD FINALLY AGREE.
THEN BLUE SHOUTED OUT, "I'LL GO FIRST. FOLLOW ME!"

HE BEGAN TO CREATE, BUT GOT CARRIED AWAY,

PAINTING RAINDROPS ALL OVER, SO THE REST COULDN'T PLAY.

THE OTHER TWO GRUMBLED, "THIS JUST ISN'T FAIR!

WE SAT HERE WAITING, WHILE YOU SPLASHED EVERYWHERE."

BUT YELLOW DECIDED TO NOT BE SO GLUM.

HE STILL WANTED TO SEE WHAT THEY ALL COULD BECOME.

SO, HE GRABBED SOME FRESH PAPER TO START SOMETHING NEW,

BUT WHEN HE BEGAN ... HE FORGOT THE REST, TOO!

HE MADE A BRIGHT SUN THAT FILLED THE WHOLE SPACE,
NOT SEEING THE FROWN THAT FORMED ON BLUE'S FACE.
"I WANTED TO PLAY, TOO," HE COMPLAINED WITH A POUT.
"BUT EACH TIME WE TRY, IT JUST DOESN'T WORK OUT.
I'M SO SORRY, RED. I KNOW THIS WAS YOUR DREAM.
BUT AS YOU CAN SEE, WE CAN'T WORK AS A TEAM."

"I KNOW THIS IS HARD," RED SAID, "BUT DON'T QUIT!

WE MUST TRY AGAIN. PLEASE GET UP, DON'T SIT.

I KNOW THIS WILL WORK, I BELIEVE IN OUR CREW!

WE'LL MAKE SOMETHING GREAT, AND WE'LL HAVE FUN TOO!"

"I'VE GOT SOME MORE PAPER," RED SMILED AND EXCLAIMED.

"WHEN WE FINISH OUR PAINTING, IT WILL SURELY GET FRAMED.

WE CAN DO SOMETHING SIMPLE! WE CAN USE ALL OUR POWERS.

HAVE YOU EVER TRIED PAINTING A GARDEN OF FLOWERS?"

YELLOW AND BLUE ALWAYS PAINTED THE SKY.

A GARDEN WAS DIFFERENT, AND THEY WERE QUITE SCARED TO TRY.

RED TRIED TO HELP AND SAID, "IT'S EASY TO DO!

IF YOU CAN PAINT CIRCLES, YOU CAN PAINT FLOWERS TOO!

EACH PETAL'S AN OVAL – A CIRCLE STRETCHED LONG,

NOW PAINT A WHOLE BUNCH. YOU JUST CAN'T GO WRONG!"

SO THEY BUILT UP THE COURAGE TO GIVE IT A SHOT.

"THIS IS EASY," BLUE SAID. "IT'S LIKE PAINTING A DOT."

YELLOW WAS PLEASED, AND HIGH-FIVED HIS FRIEND, BLUE.

AND TO THEIR SURPRISE, THEY CREATED GREEN TOO.

SOON THEY MADE ORANGE FROM YELLOW AND RED.

THEN VIOLET SHOWED, TOO, WHEN RED AND BLUE SPREAD.

NEXT CAME INDIGO, A DEEP NAVY HUE.

IT HAPPENED WHEN VIOLET DASHED QUICKLY BY BLUE.

BUT SOMETHING WAS MISSING. THE SKY WASN'T RIGHT.
IT WAS MISSING SOME COLOR. IT WAS ALL JUST SO WHITE.
SO BLUE FILLED THE SKY, AND YELLOW MADE THE SUN,
AND TOGETHER THEY CHEERED, "WOW, TEAMWORK IS FUN!"

LOOK WHAT THEY CREATED WHEN THEY ALL WORKED TOGETHER!

THE ART WAS SO BEAUTIFUL, AND IT WAS BETTER THAN EVER!

NEXT STEPS

SHOW THE FRONT COVER OF THE BOOK AGAIN. POINT TO THE AUTHOR/ILLUSTRATOR NAME. ASK THE CHILDREN IF THEY KNOW WHAT THE AUTHOR'S AND ILLUSTRATOR'S ROLES ARE IN A BOOK. DISCUSS. DO THEY KNOW ANY OTHER NAMES OF AUTHORS AND ILLUSTRATORS?

THERE ARE THREE MAIN COLORS/CHARACTERS IN THIS BOOK. NAME THEM (RED, YELLOW, BLUE). THESE ARE CALLED "PRIMARY COLORS." ASK IF THEY CAN NAME THE COLORS THAT RED AND YELLOW MAKE WHEN MIXED (ORANGE). BLUE AND YELLOW (GREEN). BLUE AND RED (PURPLE). THESE ARE CALLED "SECONDARY COLORS."

ASK THE CHILDREN TO NAME WHAT RED, BLUE, AND YELLOW PAINTED. NAME SOME ADDITIONAL THINGS THEY CAN PAINT WITH EACH COLOR. WHAT ARE SOME THINGS THEY COULD PAINT OR DRAW WITH THE SECONDARY COLORS?

AT THE BEGINNING OF THE STORY, RED, YELLOW, AND BLUE NEVER WORKED TOGETHER AS A TEAM. THEY LIKED WORKING ALONE. ASK THE CHILDREN IF THERE ARE SOME THINGS THEY PREFER DOING ALONE. WHY? ARE THERE TIMES WHEN WORKING ALONE IS BETTER?

WHAT CHANGED IN THE BOOK THAT CONVINCED RED, YELLOW, AND BLUE TO FINALLY TRY WORKING TOGETHER AS A TEAM? ASK THE CHILDREN TO NAME TIMES IN THEIR LIVES WHEN WORKING TOGETHER AS A TEAM IS BETTER.

ASK THE CHILDREN IF THEY HAVE EVER CREATED ART WITH OTHER PEOPLE. SEE IF THEY KNOW WHAT MURALS AND MOSAICS ARE. A MURAL IS ARTWORK DONE DIRECTLY ON A WALL. A MOSAIC IS A PICTURE OR PATTERN PRODUCED BY ARRANGING TOGETHER SMALL COLORED PIECES OF HARD MATERIAL, SUCH AS STONE, TILE, OR GLASS. BOTH OF THESE ARE EXAMPLES OF ART CREATED BY PEOPLE WORKING TOGETHER.

ASK THE CHILDREN IF THEY CAN THINK OF SOME TYPE OF ART THAT WOULD BE FUN TO DO WITH OTHERS. (EXAMPLES ARE SIDEWALK CHALK ART, MOSAIC, MURAL, USING BEADS, SCULPTURE.)

MAKE A LIST WITH THE CHILDREN OF ALL OF THE DIFFERENT TYPES OF ART MEDIA THEY COULD USE WHEN CREATING ARTWORK (THESE INCLUDE PAINTS, OIL PASTELS, CRAYONS, CLAY, CHALK, MARKERS, PENCILS, COLORED PENCILS.)

BRAINSTORM SOME PAINTINGS THE CHILDREN COULD MAKE THAT WOULD FEATURE ALL SIX PRIMARY AND SECONDARY COLORS. THEN LET THEM TRY IT!